Emma Entertains

EMMA FORBES

For my mother, without whose help and advice I couldn't have got this together!
And also for my godchildren Kathryn, Emily and Max.
A special thank you to Rosemary Moon, huge thanks to Mary Ellen Lamb
for doing my make-up, and to Denis at Michaeljohn for doing my hair.

First published in Great Britain in 1994 by
PAVILION BOOKS LIMITED
26 Upper Ground, London SE1 9PD

Text copyright © Emma Forbes 1994
Photographs copyright © Andrew Williams 1994
Illustrations copyright © Francis Scappaticci 1994
Home Economist: Cara Hobday

Design and art direction: Sara Kidd

All rights reserved. No part of this publication
may be reproduced, stored in a retrieval system, or
transmitted, in any form or by any means, electronic,
mechanical, photocopying, recording or otherwise,
without the prior permission of the copyright holder.

A CIP catalogue record for this book is available
from the British Library.

ISBN 1 85793 227 7

Produced by Mandarin Offset (HK) Ltd

2 4 6 8 10 9 7 5 3 1

This book can be ordered direct from the publisher. Please contact
the Marketing Department. But try your bookshop first.

CONTENTS

Top Hints and Tips for Safe Cooking
4

Introduction
5

Midnight Feast Party
6

Valentine's Day Party
12

Mother's and Father's Day Party
18

Easter Party
24

Best Birthday Ever!
30

Picnic Party
36

Sunday Brunch 'Any Excuse' Party
42

Hallowe'en Party
48

Environmentally Friendly Party
54

Boxing Day or Christmas Get-Together
58

Other Inspiring Party Ideas!
64

TOP HINTS AND TIPS FOR SAFE COOKING

1. Always use oven gloves when picking up anything that might be hot, such as a saucepan handle, or when putting anything in or taking it out of the oven.

2. When draining pasta or vegetables, take extra care with the boiling water. Put the colander down inside the sink, hold the pan well away from you, and pour slowly to avoid splashing.

3. Take great care when using sharp kitchen knives; it will ruin the recipe if you slice your fingers into it! Also, beware of the sharp blades in certain kitchen items such as food processors. You should always unplug these or switch them off at the wall, and remove the blade if you can, before removing the ingredients.

4. When frying anything in hot oil, take great care not to get too close, as hot fat can spit suddenly.

5. Never leave anything that could catch fire near the cooker.

6. The measurements in this book are all quite loosely based. A 'handful' can be as large or small as you like, and a 'cupful' means a mugful. All eggs are size 3.

7. Above all, if you are at all worried about something, or can't manage on your own, get a friend or an adult to help out – it's no fun having an accident, and it is so easy to avoid one.

INTRODUCTION

A party can be for any number of people, from two upwards (it's a little lacking in atmosphere on your own!). It's so easy to put together a party, and you can celebrate almost anything — all it takes is a little imagination. Don't always leave the organizing to other people — anyone can give a good party!

What I've collected together are some ideas for parties, celebrations and get-togethers that are a little different from the usual ones. I've also included recipes and party tips that you can do yourself rather than having to get your parents to organize or, more importantly, cook for your party! My recipes are all easy to make, they don't use too many expensive ingredients or take up too much time, and they are guaranteed to be totally delicious, leaving you plenty of time to enjoy the fun! You need only make one or two recipes from each theme — don't think that you have to make six dishes for each party, just pick and choose the ones you want.

A good tip when throwing a party is to get each guest to bring one thing, so that you don't get landed with all the work. The only downside of doing a party yourself is that you have to be responsible for the clearing up and putting away as well — get your friends to help you, and it will take half the time. Also, don't forget to ask your parents' permission before organizing any event, otherwise it could be your last party!

I wanted to think of one really brilliant tip for successful cooking, and the thing I came up with is: never be afraid of experimenting with ingredients, as you can always turn a disaster into a success. For example, if you don't have all the correct ingredients for a recipe, try something else — it may even taste better. Also, don't worry if things burn or don't look quite as you imagined. Simply use the art of disguise to cover up the messy bits and improvise using your imagination — that way you will always get end results to be proud of. Never be afraid to make up your own unique and amazing idea for a party or theme — I have given you the guidelines, so the rest is up to you!

Emma Forbes

P.S. To avoid bugging your parents too much for ingredients they might not be able to get hold of, try to pick recipes from this book according to what you have hanging around in the fridge and cupboards.

P.P.S. Unless otherwise stated, all my recipes are based on making enough for four hungry people, so just use your nut to make the recipe work for you — i.e. if you're having eight people over you'll have to double it, and if you've invited a hundred people . . . you work it out!

MIDNIGHT FEAST PARTY

I love midnight feasts; it's surprising how hungry you can be late at night, and you obviously build up your appetite by waiting. But the feast doesn't have to be eaten at midnight; sometimes it's just too difficult to wait until the stroke of twelve. When you have a midnight feast, make sure you hold it on a day when you can sleep in the next morning to recover. That way the feast could go on 'till breakfast – if you have the energy. Why not have one to celebrate the Last Day of School? Then you can really go to town!

Midnight feasts need to consist of 'snacks' that don't have to be heated up. Bear in mind that the food will be lying around on a bedroom floor, so avoid anything too messy.

INVITATIONS

Using a silver or gold pen (available from most good stationers), write the invitations on black card and decorate them with stars and moons.

THE SETTING

To get the right setting for a midnight feast, lay out lots of pillows and a large duvet that you can all sit on, and collect a few torches so that you can eat by torchlight. Don't actually eat in the bed – when you are ready to crash out, there is nothing worse than sleeping in a bed full of crumbs!

GAMES

The list of possible games to play is endless. What about 'Chinese Whispers'? It's the perfect game to play when you're attempting to keep quiet, and although it's a really simple idea, it always guarantees some laughs and funny words. Some good sayings to try are: 'Midnight feasts make magnificent, massive, munching minutes', or 'Chocoholics try to cheat by eating everyone they meet!'

If you're in the mood there is a really fun game you can play: blindfold one person and give them different things to eat while holding their nose, and see if they can guess what they are. Try a cube of raw jelly, a piece of banana or a spoonful of yogurt. You'll be surprised how well it works! If you are holding your feast at the end of term, why not compile each other's ideal school reports – the type you wish you'd got! 'Emma is a perfect and ideal student in every way – I think she will pass her French exam, without doubt, with an A (ha, ha!).'

PEANUT PITTA POCKETS

This is something that I invented to combine some of my favourite things. I adore pitta bread as it's not too heavy, and peanut butter has always been something that I could eat until it comes out of my head! You might notice it's an ingredient that sneaks into quite a few of my recipes.

INGREDIENTS

4 small round pitta bread pockets (wholemeal or plain)
4 tbsp peanut butter
1 tbsp soured cream
1 tbsp mayonnaise
2 carrots, peeled and grated
100g/4oz cream cheese
a little black pepper

Cut each pitta pocket in half and open them up. Mix the other ingredients together and spread a little inside each pocket. You can add a little sliced apple if you like. It's as easy as that and fantastically yummy!

Why is it that peanut butter sticks to the roof of your mouth? Has anyone ever come up with the answer?

Honeyed Chicken Drumsticks

These need to be made in advance, but are the ideal snack to have at any time. They are especially good for barbecues and are brilliant eaten with a jacket potato. Leave them in the fridge once you've cooked them and they've cooled, and they just taste better and better.

INGREDIENTS
8 chicken drumsticks
2 tbsp olive oil
grated rind and juice of 1 orange
2 tbsp clear honey
salt and pepper
1 tbsp grainy mustard

Preheat the oven to 180°C/350°F/Gas Mark 4.

1. Place the drumsticks in an ovenproof dish, and poke a couple of small holes in the top of each one.

2. Mix all the other ingredients together in a large bowl and blend well. Then spoon the mixture over the drumsticks, making sure each one is well covered. Bake for about 35 minutes, turning occasionally, until golden brown and well cooked. Once cooled, leave covered in the fridge.

Midnight Brownies

No feast could be called a feast in my book without including chocolate! These brownies are deliciously wicked and taste even better late at night.

INGREDIENTS
(Makes about 24 brownies)
200g/7oz plain chocolate
100g/4oz butter
175g/6oz light muscovado sugar
4 eggs
2 tbsp crunchy peanut butter
1 tsp vanilla essence
175g/6oz plain flour

Topping (optional)
bag of chocolate chips
200g/7oz packet of cream cheese
100g/4oz icing sugar

Preheat the oven to 180°C/350°F/Gas Mark 4.

1. Melt the chocolate in a heatproof bowl set over a pan of gently simmering water (be very careful). The bowl should just float, and not touch the bottom of the pan. Don't let water splash into the chocolate.

2. Beat the butter and sugar together until smooth, add the beaten eggs, bit by bit, then stir in the peanut butter and vanilla essence.

3. Fold the flour into the mixture by turning it over gently with a metal spoon and finally stir in the melted chocolate. Pour into a well-greased 23cm/9in square baking tin and bake for 20–30 minutes. Leave to cool and then cut into squares. They should be gooey and chewy.

Individual Cheesy Tartlets

Everyone is always put off at the thought of making their own pastry, but it's not that difficult. If you have a food processor, the whole thing is a breeze (though be careful not to over-process it). If you don't, just follow the instructions below.

INGREDIENTS
For the pastry
225g/8oz plain flour
150g/5oz butter or margarine
50g/2oz grated Parmesan or Cheddar cheese
2 tsp paprika (to give them a lovely colour)
2–3 tbsp ice-cold water

For the filling
You can make either one large, 2 medium or 4 small tartlets, depending on what tins you have, and can fill them with whatever you like – see the suggestions below.

Preheat the oven to 200°C/400°F/Gas Mark 6.

1. Put the flour, butter, cheese and paprika into a food processor and blend until it looks like breadcrumbs. If you are doing this by hand, chop the butter into the flour using two knives like scissors, then gently rub out the last large lumps with your fingertips. This is easiest when the butter is really cold.

2. Pour in just enough water until the dough forms a ball. Knead on a well-floured surface just until smooth. Cover with greaseproof paper and chill in the fridge for 15–20 minutes.

3. Roll out the dough thinly on a well-floured surface, and cut it to line either 1 large or 2 medium or 4 small tins. Cut the pastry bigger than the tin, then press it into the tin and gently prick the bottom a few times with a fork.

4. For a hot filling, pour the filling into the pastry case(s) and cook for about 15 minutes (small), 20 minutes (medium) and 25 minutes (large). For example, mix 2 eggs, 275ml/½ pt milk, 100g/4oz grated cheese and some chopped bacon. Or try sliced mozzarella, chopped Parma ham, 4 large tomatoes skinned and chopped, topped with pesto. For a cold filling, cook the pastry case(s) first, for the same lengths of time as above, leave to cool in the tin, then fill. Try mixing a 200g/8oz tub of cream cheese with 6 tomatoes skinned and chopped, and a handful of chopped chives; or tuna and sweetcorn mixed with mayonnaise.

Midnight Munchie Snack Sticks

This is the perfect way to eat some of your favourite things without making a huge mess or using lots of plates. You will need some of those extra long wooden cocktail sticks. You can make up your own combinations, but here are my two favourites, one savoury and one sweet.

INGREDIENTS
(Each recipe makes about 6 skewers)

For savoury snack sticks
1 packet small tortelloni, cooked
2 150g/6oz packets mozzarella, cut into cubes
1 packet cherry tomatoes
1 red, yellow or green pepper, cut into chunks

For sweet snack sticks
2 apples, chopped into chunks
2 bananas, sliced thickly
12 dried apricots
2 kiwi fruit, peeled and cut into chunks
20 grapes
squeeze of lemon (to stop fruit going brown)

This is easy to do: simply thread the food on to the sticks, using alternating bits, and lay the skewers flat on a plate. You can also make great dips to go alongside both types. For a savoury dip, simply whizz together the following: 1 clove of crushed garlic, 1 150ml/¼ pt tub of sour cream, salt and pepper to taste, 2 tbsp of dried or fresh basil and 1 heaped tbsp of mayonnaise. For the sweet dip, mix together 1 150g/5oz tub of Greek yogurt, 2 tbsp of runny honey, 1 tbsp of poppy seeds and the juice of one orange. Take a dip with each mouthful.

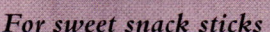

CHOCOLATE FRIDGE CAKE

Anyone who has tasted this cake knows how good it is, and also how quickly it disappears once you've made it. The greatest thing about it is that it doesn't need to be baked.

INGREDIENTS

225g/8oz plain chocolate
25g/1oz demerara sugar
100g/4oz butter
2 tbsp golden syrup
450g/1lb digestive biscuits
1 125g/4oz packet of peanuts and raisins (unsalted of course!)

1. In a bowl suspended over a pan of gently simmering water (see p. 8) put the chocolate, sugar, butter and syrup, and melt them together.

2. In another bowl, break up the biscuits into small bits and add all the peanuts and raisins.

3. Pour the melted mixture over the biscuits, nuts and raisins and stir really well. Pour into a greased 20cm/8in square cake tin.

4. Using a wooden spoon, press the mixture firmly down, then leave in the fridge until set.

N.B. You could add your own choice of ingredients to this, such as chopped up marshmallows, or chopped mixed nuts, or you could experiment using different kinds of biscuit. Remember to serve only small slices as it is incredibly rich and sickly. To decorate the cake, you can grate some extra chocolate over the top, or dust it lightly with a little icing sugar.

VALENTINE'S DAY PARTY

This is without doubt my favourite day of the year and I like to make it into a really big occasion. The shops are always crammed full of heart-shaped cards, balloons and chocolates, but no one really throws parties. Don't forget, this is one party that you can either have with the love of your life for a romantic twosome, or you can get together all of your favourite friends and relatives and make an evening to remember! Go all out on the red theme. You could ask everyone to wear either red from head to toe, or anything with a heart on it (T-shirts, brooches, earrings, etc.).

INVITATIONS

Buy some red heart-shaped balloons and some red envelopes, then simply write the time, place and message on the balloon in thick black pen, and post it in the envelope. When people receive it, they just have to blow up the balloon in order to see the message. Alternatively, you could cut out paper hearts from red tissue paper and put them inside your card to fall out of the envelope like confetti when it is opened.

GAMES

Ever heard of the saying 'to wear your heart on your sleeve'? If someone describes you as doing that, it means that you always say exactly what you feel. You could turn it into a game for a party. Make up a list of trivia questions: whoever gets the question right wins a shortbread heart, and whoever gets it wrong gets a paper heart pinned to their sleeve and has to tell something very truthful about themselves. (It could be anything from admitting to eating cold macaroni cheese for breakfast, to being madly in love with someone in the room. Could be an interesting party. . .)

Another idea is to play 'Tall Stories' – this is where one person starts to tell a story, and when they stop after a minute or so, the next person has to carry on the story in their own way. You could insist that the stories be romantic . . . Or, sit in a circle, each person taking it in turn to sing a song with the word 'love' in it. Be warned, this one could go on for ever!

FRIENDLY FISH PIE

This pie is ideal to make using any white fish such as cod or plaice. As a variation, you could use some salmon and throw a few prawns in as well, or make up your own combination of fish.

INGREDIENTS
675g/1½lb fish, cut into cubes (cod, plaice or salmon)
110g/¼lb fresh prawns (optional)
750ml/1¼pt milk
50g/2oz butter
1 small onion, finely chopped
50g/2oz cornflour
50ml/2fl oz single cream
1 large tsp English mustard
salt and pepper
1 tbsp chopped fresh dill (optional)
2 tbsp chopped fresh parsley
350g/12oz packet of frozen peas
225g/8oz ready-made shortcrust pastry
1 beaten egg, to glaze

Preheat the oven to 180°C/350°F/Gas Mark 4.

1. Put the chopped-up fish into a shallow baking dish and pour over the milk. Cover with tin foil, and bake in the oven for 10–12 minutes or until the fish is just cooked. Put the fish into a bowl and reserve the milk in a separate container.

2. Melt the butter in a large pan, and gently fry the onion until soft. Add the cornflour and stir continuously for 1–2 minutes using a whisk to help to avoid lumps.

3. Gradually pour the milk in which you poached the fish into the sauce, stirring constantly. Add the cream, mustard, salt and pepper and keep stirring until the mixture becomes smooth and thick, like custard.

4. Take the mixture off the heat and stir in the dill and parsley and taste to see if you need to add any more salt and pepper.

5. Add the peas and fish (and the prawns if you are using them) to the sauce, stir thoroughly together, and pour the mixture into a pie dish.

6. Roll out the pastry, and cut out as many hearts as you can using a knife or special heart-shaped pastry cutter. Arrange them over the top of the pie. Brush with the beaten egg and bake in the oven for 35–40 minutes, or until the sauce bubbles around the edge and the pastry is golden. Serve immediately.

Shortbread Hearts

If you don't have any ground almonds for this recipe you can always replace them with ground hazelnuts. It is a good idea to invest in a heart-shaped pastry cutter; it will always come in useful, particularly at this time of the year!

INGREDIENTS
(Makes about 12 biscuits)

100g/4oz butter
50g/2oz caster sugar
25g/1oz ground almonds
75g/3oz plain flour
50g/2oz cornflour

Preheat the oven to 180°C/350°F/Gas Mark 4.

1. Beat together the butter and sugar until light and fluffy. Add the almonds, flour and cornflour and keep stirring until the mixture sticks together.

2. Cover a surface with lots of flour, and knead the dough for 2–3 minutes. Don't over-knead – just do it until it's smooth. Then press the dough out with your hands (or use a rolling pin) until it's about 1.25cm/½in thick.

3. Using a pastry cutter, cut out as many hearts as you can. Put them on a greased baking sheet and place in the oven for 10–15 minutes or until just golden.

4. Leave to cool. They are good served with coffee, and taste delicious with a bowl of strawberries and cream.

Strawberry Sponge Cake

This is my version of the original Victoria sponge, which is a little more health-conscious than the usual recipe. I actually prefer it made with wholemeal flour as it makes the cake a bit more solid. If you are doing this for Valentine's Day, use two heart-shaped cake tins. If you have only one, bake one of the layers first using half the mixture, then when it's cooked, wash it out and use it again. Alternatively, bake two round cakes and cut into heart shapes: this makes the perfect romantic finale to the meal.

INGREDIENTS

100g/4oz margarine or butter
100g/4oz brown sugar
2 eggs, beaten
100g/4oz self-raising wholemeal flour
1 tbsp water
1 tsp vanilla essence

For the filling

100g/4oz whipping cream
100g/4oz sliced fresh strawberries
icing sugar (to taste)
2 tbsp strawberry jam

Preheat the oven to 180°C/350°F/Gas Mark 4.

1 Beat together the margarine or butter and sugar with a wooden spoon or in a food processor, add the eggs and beat well.

2 Add the flour, water and vanilla essence and beat again until light and fluffy.

3 Divide the mixture between your two greased baking tins, and put in the oven for about 20 minutes, or until risen and golden brown on top. Turn them out of the tins, and leave on a wire rack until completely cooled.

4 Whip the cream until just firm, then stir in the sliced strawberries. Add a little icing sugar to taste. Spread the jam over one of the layers, top with the cream mixture and then place the other layer on top.

5 To decorate, simply dust with a little icing sugar, or if you have any cream left over, add a few blobs of cream with a whole strawberry stuck in the middle of each.

Passion Fruit Pudding

You have to use passion fruit on Valentine's Day, purely because of its name! However, it is a delicious fruit at any time, quite an acquired taste, but extremely good when mixed with the ingredients below.

INGREDIENTS
3 ripe bananas
squeeze of lemon juice
2 ripe passion fruit
200g/7oz Greek yogurt
50g/2oz caster sugar
100g/4oz demerara sugar

1. Slice the bananas and squeeze over a little lemon juice to stop them going brown. Cut open the passion fruit, scoop out the pulp inside and add to the bananas.

2. Add the Greek yogurt and caster sugar and mix again, then divide into separate ramekin dishes or bowls.

3. Sprinkle the top of each ramekin dish with the demerara sugar, and place them under a hot grill until they are bubbling and golden brown. Leave to cool. Refrigerate for at least 2 hours and serve.

Red Jelly Terrine

This is a refreshing and light dessert that can be served in thick slices – it's not your average jelly dish! You can use different fruits, but for this party, red seems the most suitable choice.

INGREDIENTS
550ml/18fl oz blackcurrant juice
50g/2oz caster sugar
1 sachet gelatine
675g/1½lb fresh fruit e.g. red-skinned apples, cored and chopped; strawberries; raspberries; redcurrants; black grapes, cut in half with the pips removed

1. Put the blackcurrant juice and caster sugar in a small saucepan, bring to the boil, then remove from the heat. Sprinkle gelatine over 2 tbsp of cold water, stir, add to the blackcurrant juice and mix until dissolved.

2. In a loaf tin, arrange repeating layers of fruit – first a layer of apple, then strawberries and raspberries, then grapes, then apple again and so on. Pour in the jelly mixture, cover with clingfilm, and keep in the fridge until set.

3. When you are ready to serve it, simply dip the terrine in a bowl of hot water (careful not to let the water go inside the tin!), run a knife around the edges to loosen it, and then tip it out on to a plate and slice into sections.

Homemade Chocolate Truffles

Serve these straight from the fridge. Alternatively, pack them in a box between layers of greaseproof paper to make a wonderful 'edible' present for someone. You could even give a package of truffles to each of your guests as a going home present.

INGREDIENTS

100g/4oz cream cheese (not the low-fat type!)
175g/6oz icing sugar
40g/1½oz cocoa powder
50g/2oz plain chocolate
½ tsp any flavouring you like (optional) (e.g. peppermint, orange, rum, coffee, vanilla)

1. Mix together the cream cheese, icing sugar and cocoa powder in a mixing bowl, then add the flavouring if you want to.

2. Melt the chocolate – see p. 8 for how to do this. Take the bowl out and set the chocolate on one side until it has cooled slightly.

3. Mix the chocolate into the cream cheese mixture, and keep mixing it until it becomes a smooth, dark paste. Then leave the mixture in the fridge for about 10 minutes until it is still easy to shape but just starting to harden.

4. Take little pieces of the chocolate mix and roll them into balls between the palms of your hands, then roll in any of the following: cocoa powder, desiccated coconut, chopped nuts, hundreds and thousands, or chocolate vermicelli. Leave them in the fridge until they have set hard.

MOTHER'S AND FATHER'S DAY

This is the perfect opportunity for you to do something really special for either your mother or father. You don't need to make it into a party – just family is enough. Why not treat them to a wonderful, indulgent breakfast in bed with all the trimmings, which includes making their bed and doing the washing-up afterwards!

The other thing to remember when creating an 'all-stops-pulled-out' breakfast like this is to present it well. Lay a pretty napkin over the tray and then put a single flower in a small vase. You could also write out the menu on a piece of paper and decorate it to look like the real thing. Also,

include a newspaper, or perhaps a couple of favourite magazines. Don't forget that in order to do all this, you might have to get out of bed a little earlier – breakfast really needs to be served before noon!

For that perfect scrummy moment, try any of the following ideas. Although I have come up with some breakfast ideas that I know my parents would find delicious, your mother or father may like something different, so find out what their dream breakfast would be.

INVITATIONS

Leave a beautifully hand-written note stuck to the fridge the day before (check it's a day they're not too busy), warning them to stay in bed and await their surprise. To ensure that they stay put, entice them by taking up a cup of tea or coffee first so that they don't die of thirst while waiting.

RUNNY HONEY CAKE

Although cake isn't usually eaten for breakfast, this cake is very easy to make and tastes out of this world.

INGREDIENTS

100g/4oz butter
50g/2oz caster sugar
2 eggs
2 heaped tbsp natural yogurt
6 tbsp runny honey
175g/6oz plain flour
2 tsp baking powder
50g/2oz ground almonds

Preheat the oven to 180°C/350°F/Gas Mark 4.

1. Grease a 20cm/8in circular cake tin. Beat the butter and sugar together with an electric mixer or a wooden spoon until light and fluffy. Then add the eggs and the natural yogurt. Stir in 3 tbsp of the honey and mix well.

2. Mix together the flour, baking powder and ground almonds and then add to the other mixture and blend well. Spoon the mixture into the tin and bake for about 20–25 minutes, then take out of the oven, spread the remaining honey over the top and put back in the oven for 5 minutes until the cake is risen and golden or until a knife or skewer pushed right into the cake comes out clean. Then turn it out of the tin on to a wire tray to cool.

3. You can decorate this cake any way you like. My favourite is to whip a 75g/3oz carton of double cream together with 75g/3oz icing sugar and then spread it over the top of the cake (when cooled). Add lots of strawberries piled on top. Alternatively, you could ice it (why not try the Yogurt Icing on p. 34), or simply dust it lightly with a little icing sugar – whichever way you choose it's going to be a winner!

Apple Muffins

These are extremely more-ish. You can serve them warm or cold as they are, or split and spread with marmalade. If you don't finish them all off for breakfast, they make a yummy addition to your lunchbox. If you happen to be making these during the summer months, a few handfuls of fresh raspberries added to the mixture makes a great flavour combination.

INGREDIENTS
(Makes about 8–10 muffins)

275g/10oz fine wholewheat or plain flour
4tsp baking powder
¼ tsp salt
50g/2oz brown sugar
1 green or red apple, peeled and cored
75g/3oz butter
1 egg
225ml/8fl oz milk
rind of ½ lemon

Preheat oven to 220°C/425°F/Gas Mark 7.

1. Grease a muffin tin with a little butter. Put the flour, baking powder and salt into a bowl with the sugar.

2. Grate the peeled apple and stir into the above mixture. Melt the butter in a saucepan over a low heat.

3. Mix the egg, milk, lemon rind and melted butter together using a whisk, and then beat into the dry mixture, using a wooden spoon. Don't over-mix it and don't worry about any lumps!

4. Divide the mixture equally between the cups of the tin and bake for about 15–20 minutes or until risen up and golden. These delicious muffins are guaranteed to impress any parents.

Breakfast Snackjacks

I am one of those people who can eat almost anything for breakfast. I am at my most hungry the minute I wake up and I think it's important to vary what you eat. You don't have to stick to the traditional cereals and toast. Here is my recipe for 'breakfast on the run'. You could also add this to the breakfast tray for your parents – they just might get hooked.

INGREDIENTS

75g/3oz butter
2 tbsp golden syrup
75g/3oz soft brown sugar
100g/4oz rolled oats (the sort you use for porridge)
large handful of raisins
few extra oats to sprinkle over the top
1 tsp cinnamon

Preheat the oven to 180°C/350°F/Gas Mark 4.

1. Melt the butter with the golden syrup and brown sugar in a small saucepan, until it is well blended.

2. Take off the heat and mix in the oats and raisins.

3. Press into a greased 20cm/8in square baking tin (using a wooden spoon, as it will be very hot). Then bake for 15 minutes. Take out, sprinkle the remaining oats and cinnamon evenly over the top and leave to cool in the tin before chopping into squares.

Other Breakfast Suggestions....

Breakfast need never be boring, and to prove it, here are some further suggestions for things that you might like to try . . .

- **Homemade Swiss Muesli** – mix together a 500g carton of plain or fruit yogurt, and stir in 3 tbsp of porridge oats, some finely chopped and peeled apple, a handful of raisins and a spoonful of honey (only if it is a plain yogurt) – serve in a bowl topped with some sliced banana.

- **Cinnamon Toast** – butter a slice of toast, then sprinkle over a little caster sugar and a small sprinkling of cinnamon.

- **Scrambled Egg Sandwich** – spread a slice of toast with some tomato ketchup, top with a layer of scrambled egg, and then place a buttered slice of toast on top (this sandwich needs to be eaten with a knife and fork!!)

Grapefruit Salad

This is really just a plain old fruit salad, using any fruit you happen to have in the house, but presented in half a grapefruit to make it look more interesting. Alternatively, you could use half a melon. Simply halve the grapefruit and scoop out the middle, then mix together any fruit you like before filling the half skin up. Sprinkle a little brown sugar and cinnamon over the top as well.

Breakfast Baskets

INGREDIENTS
4 slices of brown or white bread
a little butter
4 eggs
2 tbsp milk
salt and pepper
2 large tomatoes
50g/2oz grated Cheddar cheese

Preheat the oven to 200°C/400°F/Gas Mark 6.

1. Cut the crusts off the bread and spread both sides with butter. Then press each slice into a muffin tin. Place in the oven for about 10 minutes, or until they look golden and crisp.

2. Melt a little butter in a saucepan over a low heat. Whisk together the eggs, milk, salt and pepper in a bowl. Then scramble the eggs in the butter over a low heat, stirring constantly with a wooden spoon until done to your liking.

3. Divide the egg mixture evenly between the four toast cups. Add half a tomato to each one, and sprinkle a little grated cheese over the top. Place under a hot grill for about 5 minutes until bubbling.

EASTER PARTY

As far as most people are concerned, Easter is the time to eat as many chocolate eggs, bunnies and sweets as possible, and they usually end up feeling ill and spotty. I get quite sick of Easter egg chocolate after a while (normally after about 10 eggs!), and have always wished that I could do something else with it, so I've come up with a really good idea to use up that leftover chocolate. If you do decide to have an Easter get-together, make sure you organize a traditional Easter egg hunt. Work out all the clues carefully beforehand, and hide the eggs well. To avoid disappointment for younger members of the family, remember to make a few of them a little bit more obvious.

INVITATIONS

Cut an Easter egg shape out of some cardboard. Decorate it as imaginatively as you like and write your message on the back.

GAMES

Make your own Easter bonnet – get everyone to bring along a hat, of any description, and a pair of scissors. Give everyone exactly half an hour to decorate their hat, using beads, ribbons and so on, or wild flowers and leaves from the garden. Don't use your parents' beautiful prize-winning blooms or Easter could turn into a disaster!

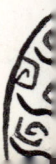

Leftover Easter Egg Choc-Chip Cookies

What could be a better way to use up that leftover Easter egg chocolate than by crumbling big chunks into this biscuit dough mix. For some reason, Easter chocolate always tastes better (I think!) than normal chocolate, so it makes these cookies taste extra delicious. However, if you're making them at any other time of the year, just use 2–3 bags of any colour chocolate chips.

INGREDIENTS
(Makes about 20–25 cookies)
175g/6oz butter
100g/4oz caster sugar
50g/2oz demerara or muscovado sugar
1 egg
½ tsp vanilla essence
225g/8oz plain flour
1 tsp baking powder
2 tbsp milk
175g/6oz crumbled chocolate

Preheat the oven to 180°C/350°F/Gas Mark 4.

1. Beat the butter and both sugars together in a bowl with a wooden spoon, then add the egg and vanilla essence and beat until light and fluffy.

2. Add the flour and baking powder, then the milk, and beat until well combined.

3. Stir in the chocolate, then wrap the mixture in greaseproof paper and leave to chill in the fridge for about 15 minutes. Unwrap and break off small teaspoonfuls and place on to a greased baking sheet (make sure they are placed well apart as they spread in the oven!). You will need at least 2 baking sheets.

4. Bake for 12–15 minutes, or until golden and slightly puffed up, then place on a wire rack to cool.

Easter Basket Case Cake

You won't become a basket case getting this ready for your party! All you have to do is to choose one of the following cake recipes from this book: either the Soggy Chocolate Birthday Cake, the Strawberry Sponge Cake (without the strawberries!), the Runny Honey Cake, or the Lemon, Banana and Poppy Seed Pound Cake. Bake your chosen cake in a circular 20cm/8in cake tin.

INGREDIENTS
1 cooked cake (see above)
3–4 cupfuls of fresh fruit
½ lemon
150g/5fl oz whipping cream
icing sugar

1. When you have cooked and cooled your cake, cut the middle out, leaving 5cm/2in around the edge. Don't throw the middle away, you'll need it later. Chop up the fresh fruit – any you like, although it would be nice to use some quite exotic fruits if you can get them. Squeeze the juice of half a lemon over the fruit and set it to one side. Whip up the cream with a little icing sugar to taste.

2. Just before you are about to serve the cake, stir the fruit in with the cream and then pile it all up in the middle of the cake. It doesn't matter if it overflows, as it's meant to look like a basket. Then balance on the top the middle that you cut out, and there you have it!

Filo Parcels

Filo pastry is very easy to use, and always gives an impressive result. It's also much lighter and lower in fat than other types of pastry, so is a bit better for you. Try using it for other recipes where pastry is required. I have given you my favourite filling for these parcels, but feel free to experiment yourself with other mixtures (the mixture for the Stuffed Pasta Shells on p. 40 also works well as a filling).

INGREDIENTS

75g/3oz butter
3 tbsp chutney
2 apples, peeled, cored and grated
100g/4oz Cheddar cheese
1 packet of filo pastry

Preheat the oven to 180°C/350°F/Gas Mark 4.

1. Melt the butter in a small saucepan over a low heat.

2. Mix together the chutney, grated apple and cheese in a bowl, and set aside.

3. Lay out your pastry sheets and cover with a damp cloth until you need them. You will need 2 sheets per parcel. Using a pastry brush, spread the first sheet with a little of the melted butter, then place the next sheet on top. Do the same again, and then put a large heaped tablespoon of the mixture in the middle of the square. Spread a little butter all around the mixture and then scrunch all four corners together to form a parcel. Brush a little more butter over the top and then place on a greased baking tray.

4. Bake until the parcels go brown. The time depends on the size you make your parcels; if you decide to make tiny ones, they will take only about 5 minutes to cook, but if you make bigger ones they could take up to 10 minutes.

Cinnamon Raisin Roll-up Muffins

These are so simple to make, yet they look as if they were made in a bakery. People will be incredibly impressed by your baking expertise . . . little will they know! Cinnamon is a spice that is used in many traditional Easter cakes and goodies, so here is a different way of using it.

INGREDIENTS
(Makes about 8 muffins)

4 heaped tsp cinnamon
3 heaped tbsp caster sugar
2 handfuls of raisins
50g/2oz butter
50g/2oz caster sugar
1 egg
225g/8oz self-raising flour
2 tsp baking powder
1 tsp salt
2–3 tbsp milk (plus extra for glazing)

Preheat the oven to 180°C/350°F/Gas Mark 4.

1. In a small bowl, mix together the cinnamon, caster sugar and raisins. Set on one side.

2. In a mixing bowl, beat together the butter and sugar with a wooden spoon then add the egg.

3. Mix together the dry ingredients, the flour, baking powder and salt, and add them to the egg mixture bit by bit. Slowly pour in the milk, using only just enough to bind the mixture together into a ball.

4. Flour a surface really well (this mixture is extremely sticky!) and gently knead the dough. Use plenty of flour on your hands and knead for a couple of minutes, or until the mixture becomes smooth. Then roll or pat the mixture out into a long rectangle.

5. Using a spoon, spread the raisin mixture evenly over the top, making sure the whole area is generously coated. Then roll up the rectangle away from you to make a Swiss-roll shape.

6. Grease a muffin tin with a little butter, then cut the roll into 7.5cm/3in slices and place each slice in a muffin cup, with the spiral bit facing up. Brush with a little milk and put in the oven.

7. Bake for 20–25 minutes, or until the muffins have risen up and gone golden brown, and the smell of the cinnamon is overpowering. Take out of the oven and serve them warm in a basket. Watch them disappear!

TOTALLY DIFFERENT EGG SANDWICHES

I love egg sandwiches, but no one ever seems to be very inventive with them, and they are nearly always made with cress. Mine have a really different 'bite' to them that I think you will agree makes them unique.

INGREDIENTS
6 hard-boiled eggs
1 packet watercress
salt and pepper
1 tsp Dijon or English mustard
4 tbsp mayonnaise
butter or margarine
8 slices of any bread you like, or 4 baps or rolls

Finely chop the egg and watercress and mix together with the salt, pepper, mustard and mayonnaise in a large bowl. Butter your bread and fill each sandwich with a big portion of the mixture. Cover and keep in the fridge until serving.

N.B. Watercress has a very strong peppery taste. You could use chopped tomato instead, if you prefer something milder, (but your sandwich won't then be totally different!).

BEST BIRTHDAY EVER!

Traditionally, your parents give you a party on your birthday; they organize everything, do the invitations, make all the food, bake the cake and arrange the games and going-home presents, as well as making the house look great. However, this is the busy 90s; parents are often working and could use a break! So why not move with the times, and throw, or at least help throw, your own party? You might enjoy organizing it so much you end up doing all the parties in your household, for brothers, sisters and friends. You can make it as elaborate or as simple as you like, and either make it a solo effort, or rope in a few friends as slaves!

INVITATIONS

The invitations really depend on what style of party you are throwing. You could photocopy the person's birth certificate and send it out with the message on the back.

(Don't do this for your parents – they'd never forgive you!) Perhaps you could find a really funny baby picture of yourself or the person whose birthday it is, and photocopy that with the details written underneath. It's up to you!

Games

Try pass the parcel, which should be wrapped in layers of newspaper, but include forfeits such as making a dress out of a paper bag, acting out a beauty commercial, singing one of the latest chart hits, or the best one – swapping clothes with the person on your left. Another fun idea is to compile a 'This is Your Life' book about the person whose birthday it is. Fill a scrap-book with photos, memorabilia, friends' comments, perhaps a photo of their favourite movie star and so on. Not only would you have a lot of laughs putting it together, it would also be a unique present.

Passionate About Pasta, Pasta

This is especially for all those of you who are as passionate about pasta as I am. It's ideal for serving at a birthday party, because a little goes a long way.

INGREDIENTS
4 tbsp olive oil
1 large onion, finely chopped
1 clove of garlic, finely chopped
10 rashers of streaky bacon, chopped
2 cupfuls of broccoli florets
1 packet of dried tagliatelle
4 tbsp single cream
2 tbsp grated Parmesan
salt and pepper

1 Heat the oil in a frying pan, and add the onion and garlic and bacon, and fry until cooked. Then add the broccoli and keep cooking for a further 3–4 minutes until the broccoli is just cooked through, but not overdone.

2 Drop the pasta into a large pan of salted boiling water and cook for about 6–8 minutes, until just cooked. Drain and put in a large serving bowl.

3 Pour the sauce over the pasta, add the cream and Parmesan, and toss everything together. Add salt and pepper to taste, and serve immediately. Then just let everyone dig in.

Crunchy Chicken or Turkey Peanut Goujons

These make the ideal party food as they can be prepared in advance, are delicious hot or cold, are full of healthy ingredients and make a good high-protein snack. You can use either chicken or turkey, or a combination of both.

Goujons were originally made with small French fish called gudgeons, coated in breadcrumbs (that's how this recipe got its name).

INGREDIENTS
4 slices wholemeal bread, made into breadcrumbs
4 tbsp peanut butter
1 tsp black pepper
2 eggs
4 chicken or turkey breasts (approx. 450g/1lb), skinned and boned

Preheat the oven to 190°C/375°F/Gas Mark 5.

1. Mix the breadcrumbs with the peanut butter and black pepper. This is easiest done in a food processor, but if you don't have one, just do it in a large bowl with a fork.

2. Lightly beat the two eggs together in a bowl. Slice the chicken or turkey into strips, and dip them first into the egg, and then into the breadcrumb/peanut butter mixture, making sure each piece is really well covered.

3. Line a baking sheet with tin foil, and put the chicken pieces on the sheet, well spread out, and bake until the coating is golden brown and the chicken is cooked through (about 15–20 minutes – test one by cutting it in half and looking inside). Serve with a homemade dip such as Skinny Dip (see recipe below).

Skinny Dip

INGREDIENTS
1 150ml/5fl oz pot natural yogurt
2 tbsp mayonnaise
salt and pepper
fresh chopped chives

Mix together the yogurt with the mayonnaise, then add a little salt and pepper, and either a handful of fresh chopped chives or 2 tbsp of dried chives or mint or parsley – that's it!

This dip tastes good with all kinds of accompaniments, such as sticks of celery, strips of carrots or pieces of raw cauliflower.

Brilliant Bruschettas

'Bruschettas' are really just toasted bread, topped with different things and then grilled – they are almost like a different style of pizza . . . a bit like miniature pizzas.

INGREDIENTS

1 loaf of either sourdough or ciabatta bread (both available in supermarkets or Italian delis) or a French baguette
olive oil (you don't need measurements, it's just to drizzle over)
6 large tomatoes, peeled and chopped
2 × 150g/6oz packets of mozzarella, chopped
2 tsp dried oregano
salt and pepper
6 black pitted olives, chopped (if you like them!)
1 clove of garlic, crushed

1. Take your loaf of bread and cut it into thick slices. Place them on a baking tray, and drizzle a little olive oil on to each slice, just enough to cover (don't overdo it!). Place them under a hot grill for 2–3 minutes, turn over and repeat on the other side.

2. In another bowl, mix together all the other ingredients. To peel tomatoes, simply place them in a bowl, prick the skins with a knife, then pour some boiling water from the kettle over them. Leave for 2 minutes, drain, and then you'll find the skin will come away easily.

3. Spoon the mixture over the toast, dividing it between each slice, drizzle over a little more olive oil, and place back under the grill until bubbling. Serve hot or cold.

Fruit Coulis and Ice-Cream

Get in 2 or 3 of your favourite flavours of ice-cream, and make a couple of these fruit coulis (a fine purée) to go with each scoop. You can use whatever fruit happens to be in season, but it works best with strawberries or raspberries because of their great colour. All you have to do is whizz up the fruit in a blender with icing sugar to taste, then press the pulp through a sieve using a spoon, and it's ready in two seconds to eat with your ice-cream.

Soggy Chocolate Birthday Cake

I can promise you that everyone will love this cake — even though I say so myself, it is the best chocolate cake ever. It doesn't come out too spongy as it contains natural yogurt, which makes it nice and moist, but be careful not to overcook it. It is also really easy to prepare, especially if you have a food processor, because you can put everything in together.

INGREDIENTS

175g/6oz butter
225g/8oz self-raising flour
40g/1½oz cocoa powder
175g/6oz caster sugar
¼ tsp salt
2 eggs
½ tsp vanilla essence
225g/8oz natural yogurt

Preheat the oven to 180°C/350°F/Gas Mark 4.

1. In a small saucepan, melt the butter over a low heat and set aside.

2. In a large mixing bowl, mix together all the dry ingredients: flour, cocoa powder, sugar and salt. Then stir in the eggs, vanilla essence and melted butter.

3. Finally add the yogurt and beat until the mixture becomes a smooth batter (don't over-beat). Pour into a greased 20cm/8in baking tin and bake for 25–30 minutes, or until a knife comes out clean when inserted into the middle. If there are any gooey bits, leave it a few minutes longer.

4. Leave to cool before turning it out on to a wire rack.

Yogurt Icing

Beat together 225g/8oz icing sugar, with 100g/4oz cocoa powder, and add just enough natural yogurt to get it to the consistency you like, then spread over the top. You will need to cover the cake and keep it in the fridge once it has been iced.

To decorate the cake, you can either keep it simple — or you can go for the O.T.T. version and cover it in a mass of jelly babies, chocolate buttons, smarties or anything you like. Whatever else you do, don't forget the candles. However, if the birthday person is over 30, my advice is just stick to one candle!

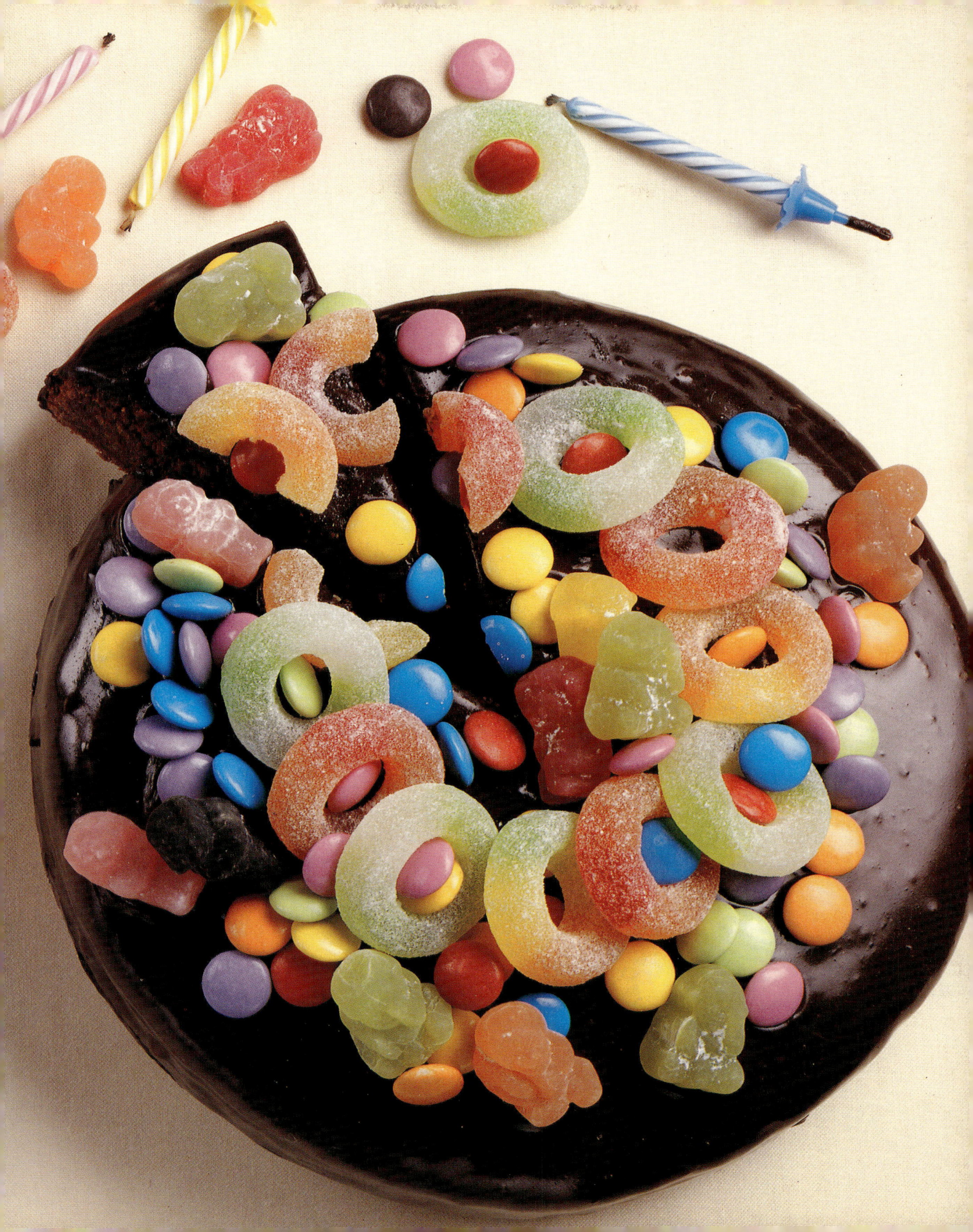

PICNIC PARTY

Everyone loves a picnic, and yet we rarely have them because of the unpredictable weather. Of course they're best of all on a hot summer's day, but don't panic – always be prepared for rain, and just bring the picnic indoors – it'll still be as much fun snacking on the floor. The most important thing to remember if the weather is hot is to keep all the food cool. Unless you have a cool box, make sure that you take with you only things that don't mind a bit of heat and won't give you food poisoning to remember the day by! Here's my list of things to avoid on a hot summer's day, *unless* you have the proper cooling system.

1. Chicken
2. Fish or shellfish
3. Eggs
4. Yogurts and cheese products

Also, remember to wrap things like sandwiches in greaseproof paper, and use plastic containers for salads, etc.

Don't worry though, there is still plenty of scope to create some extra-yummy things that will make any onlooking picnickers green with envy. A good day to have a picnic is 'Midsummer Day' on 24th June – at least you stand a chance that the weather might be good!

INVITATIONS

Draw a red-and-white checked tablecloth on a piece of paper and write on the top of it in a bright colour, asking each person to bring something useful along with them: for example, paper plates, napkins, plastic knives, forks and spoons, packets of crisps, a football, a frisbee, etc.

Heat oven to 180°C/350°F/Gas Mark 4.

1. Brush each layer of filo pastry with melted butter and a little marmite. Sprinkle each layer with fresh or dried herbs, grated cheese and salt and pepper.

2. Slice into 5cm/2in strips, lay them on a greased baking tray and bake for about 10–12 minutes.

You can use almost any bits and pieces to flavour these, as long as they're small or finely chopped: try crushed garlic, a little curry powder or parmesan cheese.

Filo Cheesy Straws

INGREDIENTS
1 packet filo pastry
melted butter
marmite
fresh or dried herbs
50g/2oz Cheddar cheese

Inventive Hoagies

I'm not sure where the word 'hoagies' came from, but it simply refers to very big rolls, ideal for extremely hungry people. Don't be boring with your fillings though (sandwiches need never be boring); here are just a few delicious and tempting examples of what you could be biting into.

- turkey with cream cheese and pear
- avocado with sour cream and bacon
- peanut butter with honey and banana
- mozzarella, sun-dried tomato and peppers
- tofu, avocado and tahini (available from health-food shops)
- grated carrot, apple, raisins and mayonnaise
- chocolate spread with sliced bananas
- cheese, pickle and apple slices

A Picnic Citrus Tart

This is so good and easy to make, and it always reminds me of lazy summer days, so it's perfect for a picnic.

INGREDIENTS

For the crust
225g/8oz digestive biscuits (or ginger biscuits), crushed into crumbs
2 tbsp caster sugar
75g/3oz melted butter

For the filling
3 eggs
50g/2oz melted butter
100g/4oz caster sugar
2 large lemons
1 orange
1 lime

Preheat the oven to 180°C/350°F/Gas Mark 4.

1. For the crust, simply combine the crust ingredients in a bowl, and press firmly down into a 20cm/8in pie dish using your fingertips, making it as flat as you can. Leave on one side.

2. Mix the eggs, melted butter and caster sugar together in a bowl. Grate in about 2 tbsp of rind from the lemons, orange and lime, saving a little extra rind for decoration. Add the juice of the 2 lemons, the orange and the lime.

3. Pour the mixture over the biscuit crust and bake for 20–25 minutes, until it looks golden and toffee-like. Take out, leave to cool, then keep in the fridge. Serve with some whipped cream, or Greek yogurt and honey.

4. To decorate, simply sprinkle the rest of the rind over the top and dust with icing sugar. It would look really stunning served on a huge plate, or a flat basket tray with a base of green leaves.

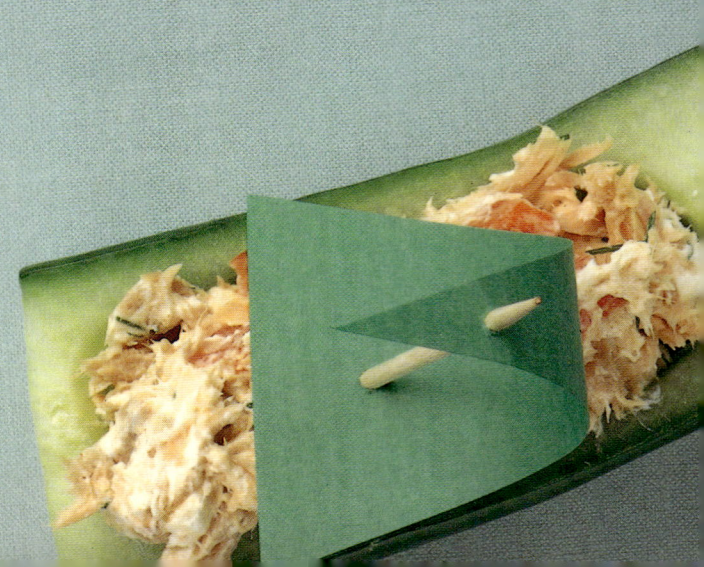

Filled-up Cucumbers

Ideal as a snack, either for the picnic, or as an interesting addition to your lunchbox.

INGREDIENTS
1 large cucumber (as straight as possible!)
100g/4oz cream cheese
½ red pepper, finely chopped
salt and pepper
½ tsp cayenne pepper
1 tbsp fresh dill, chopped
squeeze of lemon juice
99g/3½oz can of tuna, drained

1. Chop off the ends of the cucumber, then slice the whole cucumber in half along its length. This is tricky – get someone to hold it firmly as you cut, and keep fingers out of the way. Using a teaspoon, gently scoop the middle out of each half (the squidgy bit with the pips in).

2. Mix all the other ingredients together in a bowl, and fill each half of the cucumber, pressing as much in as you can. Cover and keep in the fridge until you need it. Any leftover mixture makes a great dip for crackers, crisps or crudités (chopped-up raw vegetables). Or you could stuff something else – a whole red or green pepper, sticks of celery, etc.

Stuffed Pasta Shells

These can be eaten cold on a picnic, but they are also good served hot with a fresh tomato sauce as a delicious main course for a special dinner. The extra large pasta shells shouldn't be too difficult to get hold of. Serves 4–6 hungry people.

INGREDIENTS
8 giant dried pasta shells
butter
1 tbsp olive oil
1 onion, finely chopped
2 cloves of garlic, finely chopped
12 large spinach leaves
2 tomatoes, chopped
salt and pepper
250g/9oz ricotta cheese
2 tsp dried or fresh basil
50g/2oz grated Parmesan

Preheat the oven to 180°C/350°F/Gas Mark 4.

1. Cook the pasta shells in a large pan of salted boiling water for about 10 minutes or until just cooked. Drain and rinse them under cold water and set to one side in a large, shallow, ovenproof dish that you have greased with some butter. Try to keep their shape as much as possible, and handle carefully, as they tear easily.

2. Heat the olive oil in a frying pan, add the onion and garlic, and cook for a couple of minutes over a medium heat until soft. Chop up the spinach leaves (take off the stalks first), and add the spinach and tomatoes to the pan with a little salt and pepper. Cook until it becomes mushy.

3. Take off the heat, and transfer to a mixing bowl. Add in the ricotta cheese and the basil and give it a really good stir.

4. This is the fun bit – using a small spoon, fill each shell with the mixture and sprinkle a little Parmesan over each one. Bake in the oven for 10 minutes, or until heated through.

Crunchy Salad in a Bag

INGREDIENTS
6 stems celery, chopped
1 packet of beansprouts
2 apples, cored and chopped
juice of ½ lemon
salt and pepper
4 large carrots, peeled and chopped
1 handful of raisins

Putting salad in a bag is the best way to make sure you don't arrive on your picnic with a soggy salad. Take along your favourite salad dressing in a separate bottle or container and put all the chopped-up salad stuff in a large plastic bag. When you're ready to serve, pour the dressing into the bag, hold on to the top, shake well and *voilà*!

Parmesan Pasta

INGREDIENTS
500g/1lb either penne or spiral pasta
4 tbsp olive oil
4 heaped tbsp grated Parmesan cheese
10 cherry tomatoes
2 tsp fresh or dried basil
salt and pepper
1 tbsp balsamic vinegar (or use a squeeze of lemon juice instead)
150g/5oz mozzarella or feta cheese, cut into chunks
50g/2oz Cheddar cheese, cut into chunks

1. Drop the pasta into a large pan of salted boiling water, and cook for about 10 minutes, or until just tender. Drain in a colander, rinse with cold water and put into a bowl, stir in the olive oil and leave to cool.

2. Mix all the remaining ingredients together with the pasta and chill in the fridge until you need it.

Honey Mustard Dressing

INGREDIENTS
4 tbsp olive oil
1 tbsp vinegar
1 tsp runny honey
pinch of salt
pinch of pepper
1 tbsp grainy mustard

The best way is to put all the ingredients in an empty jam jar (clean of course!). Put the lid on tightly and shake it really well, and keep in the fridge until you need it. You can also add a peeled clove of garlic in the bottom to give it extra flavour.

SUNDAY BRUNCH 'ANY EXCUSE' PARTY

Sunday is traditionally a day of peace and quiet in some households. The object of this party is to keep yourselves amused on a dull Sunday without causing your parents too much hassle and while also managing to remain relatively quiet. You could make this a productive party, a time to do some creative things while also having a good time and eating some easy-to-put-together dishes. The reason I also call it an 'Any Excuse' party is because you don't need to celebrate anything in particular – this is one of those last-minute ideas for that weekend when you've nothing better to do.

INVITATIONS

Cut out individual letters, funny headlines and pictures from old copies of the Sunday papers, and make up your own unique and witty invitations to send out, by sticking all the bits on to pieces of plain card.

GAMES

A Sunday brunch party is not the time to rush around like a maniac, so why not get each friend to bring round their favourite board game, and organize huge championships and heats. Alternatively, get each friend to bring round any scraps and pieces of junk they have lying around that would make a brilliant collage. Someone needs to provide a huge piece of card to stick it all on, along with some glue, scissors and so on, but everyone can contribute to making what could potentially be a very valuable piece of modern art!

Pick-me-up Shake

If you've got that Sunday feeling, this could be the ideal pick-me-up tonic. Most milkshakes can be a bit too sickly, but you can make some really refreshing drinks that are also good for you.

INGREDIENTS
(Makes enough for 2 tall glasses)

1 ripe banana, chopped
handful of fresh or frozen raspberries (thawed) or a handful of strawberries
550ml/1pt semi-skimmed milk
150g/5oz fruit yogurt or Greek yogurt with honey
½ tsp cinnamon
juice of 1 orange (or 2 tbsp fresh orange juice)
any 2 pieces of fruit, roughly chopped into small pieces

Put everything except your chosen 2 pieces of fruit into a food processor or electric blender and whizz until frothy. Pour into 2 tall glasses and leave to chill in the fridge for about half an hour. Just before serving, add the remaining fruit to the top of each drink, stick a spoon and a straw into each glass then give the drink a stir and serve immediately.

You could invent your own 'speciality of the house', perhaps something quite exotic, depending on what fruits you have; for example, a mango whizzed up with Greek yogurt, or a little apple juice and a kiwi fruit can make you feel as if you are on holiday somewhere tropical!

Mega Meatloaf

This is a great recipe for doing something a little different with mince. We've all had hamburgers and shepherd's pie, but this is more unusual, and tastes really good both hot and cold. I think it is best served with a steaming hot jacket potato and a mixed salad, but you could also serve slices of cold meatloaf, with a spoonful of pickle, between two pieces of bread for a really 'alternative' sandwich.

INGREDIENTS

450g/1lb lean minced beef
2 slices wholemeal bread made into breadcrumbs
1 small onion, very finely chopped
1 tbsp dried mixed herbs
pinch of salt
pinch of black pepper
1 tbsp tomato purée
2 eggs
1 tbsp Worcestershire sauce
50g/2oz sliced mozzarella, or grated Cheddar cheese
1 heaped tbsp tomato ketchup (optional)

Preheat the oven to 180°C/350°F/Gas Mark 4.

1. Simply combine all of the above (except the cheese and tomato ketchup) in a large mixing bowl, until really well mixed.

2. Using your hands, pat the mixture out on to a sheet of greaseproof paper or tin foil, to make an oblong shape about 2.5cm/1in thick. Then fold one side over, using the paper to help guide you, and keep rolling until it forms a jam roll shape.

3. Press together any gaps and cracks and, using the paper to lift it, place it on to a lined baking tray. Cover the whole thing with a sheet of tin foil and bake in the oven for about 45 minutes.

4. When the loaf is cooked, take out and unwrap. Make several cuts along the top and sprinkle on the cheese and a little tomato ketchup if you like. Put it back in the oven for a further 5 minutes, or until the cheese has melted and is golden and bubbling.

The Great Brunch Bake

Your mother will love you for this one – it's your chance to use up all the leftovers from the weekend in one scrummy dish that everyone can enjoy. Although I give a list of ingredients here, you can vary them depending on what is in your fridge. This will also fill the tummies of any vegetarians you know who might not want to eat meatloaf.

INGREDIENTS

1 225g/½lb packet any dried pasta shapes (bows, spirals, shells, etc.)
3 tbsp olive oil
1 clove garlic, crushed
1 onion, finely chopped
1 large tin chopped tomatoes
1 tbsp tomato ketchup
1 tsp brown sugar
a few leaves of fresh basil, chopped, or 2 heaped tsp dried basil
salt and black pepper
1 chicken stock cube dissolved in 150ml/¼pt hot water
2 cupfuls of any leftover vegetables, such as peas, carrots, courgettes, broccoli, onions or potatoes, chopped up

Preheat the oven to 190°C/375°F/Gas Mark 5.

1. In a large saucepan, drop the pasta into salted boiling water and cook for about 10 minutes until *al dente*, which means until *just* done. Drain, rinse with cold water and leave on one side.

2. In large saucepan, heat the olive oil and cook the garlic and chopped onion until soft and transparent. Then add the tinned tomatoes, tomato ketchup, brown sugar, basil, salt and pepper and water with a stock cube dissolved in it, and simmer for about 5 minutes.

3. Mix together the leftover chopped vegetables, pasta and the tomato sauce really well, before putting into an ovenproof dish. Cover with the grated cheese and place in the oven for about 20 minutes until bubbling, and then if you like, put it under a hot grill for a further 5 minutes to make the top go crunchy and golden.

This is a meal in itself. If you want to serve anything with it, just a plain green salad will do.

Easy Lumpy Apple Batter Cake

If you are going to have a really lazy Sunday, sitting in front of a log fire, what could be nicer at 4 o'clock than a huge mug of tea and a slice of delicious cake. If you have friends round for a brunch party, a cup of tea and cake could be just what the doctor ordered if a game of Monopoly or Scrabble is getting very heated and competitive.

INGREDIENTS

4 eating apples, peeled, cored and chopped
200g/8oz brown or muscovado sugar
1 egg
35ml/1½fl oz sunflower oil
1 handful of raisins
100g/4oz plain flour
½ tsp salt
1 tsp baking powder
1 tsp cinnamon
½ tsp ground ginger

Preheat the oven to 180°C/350°F/Gas Mark 4.

1. Mix up the apples and sugar in a mixing bowl using a wooden spoon, then add the egg and the oil. Mix it all around until well blended. Then add the raisins.

2. Put the flour, salt, baking powder, cinnamon and ginger in the bowl, and fold them into the apple mixture.

3. Pour the mixture into a greased 20cm/8in sandwich tin (you can use any shape you like) and bake for about 1 hour 10 minutes. You can tell it's done by sticking a knife in carefully and seeing if it comes out clean.

4. To decorate, cut and quarter an apple, and scoop out the core. Then cut the quarters in half again. In a small saucepan, melt together the juice of 1 lemon and 2 tbsp orange or lemon marmalade and a little knob of butter. Gently heat the apple slices in the mixture, making sure each section is well coated. Then, using a fork, arrange them neatly on the top of your cake.

BLINIS OR BABY PANCAKES

What better day to attempt pancakes than a Sunday, when you've got all the time in the world to pick them up off the floor and start again! Blinis are smaller and fatter than normal pancakes, and they make a wonderful pudding, or can be served for your brunch. They are also delicious to have on a plate as a snack while watching a video. The good thing about blinis is that you don't have to toss them; simply flip them over using a spatula. Take turns to cook them, as people always want more than one, and you don't want to be the person stuck with the frying pan the whole time! It's a good idea to lay out lots of different fillings, so that people can just take their blini and fill it as they like with chopped ham, cheese, mozzarella, sliced tomatoes, bananas, ice-cream – you name it!

INGREDIENTS

For the basic batter
100g/4oz plain flour
pinch of salt
1 egg, beaten
275ml/½pt milk
25g/1oz butter, melted
a little sunflower oil for frying

To make the mixture unique, add any of the following combinations to the batter mixture:
2 mashed ripe bananas, plus ½ tsp cinnamon
75g/3oz cocoa powder plus 2 tbsp caster sugar
75g/3oz grated Cheddar cheese plus a handful of fresh spinach leaves, roughly chopped

1. Simply heat up a little oil in your frying pan and add a couple of large tablespoonfuls of mixture to the pan, or enough to cover the bottom. Cook for 2–3 minutes on one side before attempting to flip it over. Each blini should be about 7cm/3in across.

2. To serve, you can either roll them up, serve them flat on a plate, or if you cut out some squares of greaseproof paper, you can serve them folded in a sheet of paper, so that people can eat them in their hands.

3. Always have a few wicked fillings lying around that you can add to your blinis – maple syrup, chocolate sauce, vanilla ice-cream, lemon juice, etc. – but not all together! People have the weirdest favourite concoctions, so don't forget to be creative and make up your own.

HALLOWE'EN PARTY

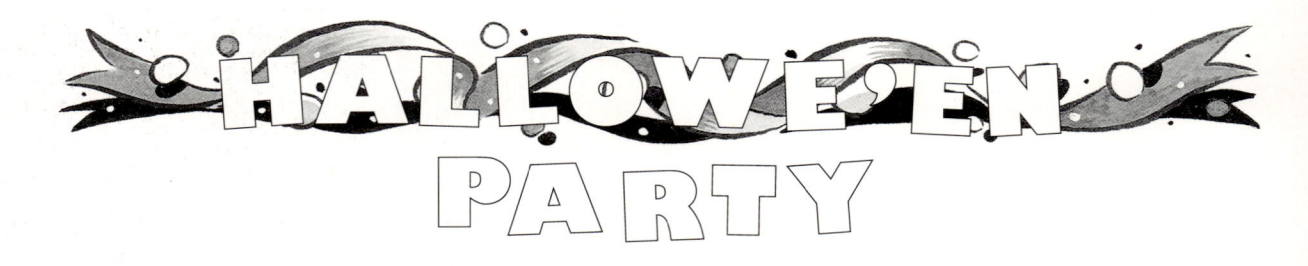

Hallowe'en is one of the dates of the year when you can really go to town – dressing-up, making horrible monster masks, playing scary games and reading spooky stories. A word of caution: this is also a day to have FUN, so don't freak yourself out too much. There's nothing fun about being scared out of your wits.

The two things you need to invest in for this occasion are a bottle of black food dye (available from all good party shops), and a big bag of jelly worms (edible ones only please!) which you can use to decorate the top of the Lemon, Banana and Poppy Seed Pound Cake (see p. 50).

INVITATIONS

Cut out some simple mask shapes from stiff white card. Make a hole in each side, and thread a piece of ribbon through each hole to tie around your head. Then just write your message, the time, date and place of the party on the back, and when your guests arrive, you can all decorate your masks. Get everyone to bring along their own paints, colours, stickers, etc. You could also, if you don't mind spending a little bit more money, buy packets of pumpkin seeds and write the party details on the back. Put them in an envelope and post them, and then people could plant the seeds and, who knows, next year's party could host a 'who has grown the biggest pumpkin' competition!

You could make 'goody bags' for people to take home, full of the sorts of thing you might get if you went out 'trick or treating' – satsumas, sweets, jokes, tricks, and so on.

DECORATIONS

You need a dark room to make the atmosphere as scary as possible. Try making tents to sit in by looping sheets or blankets over chairs and light them from the inside using torches – it will give a really weird effect. If you are the possessor of a proper tent, set it up indoors with a notice saying 'Enter at your own risk – House of Horror'.

CAULDRON CASSEROLE

This dish is so easy to make, yet it is very impressive and tastes wonderful. If you want to try this with another meat, use some lean lamb, cut into chunks. It works really well with the rosemary.

**INGREDIENTS
(Serves 4–6)**

2 tbsp plain flour
6 chicken thighs, skinned and boned
3 tbsp sunflower oil
2 leeks, chopped
1 onion, peeled and chopped into quarters
2 large carrots, chopped
500g/1lb baby new potatoes
425g/15oz tin flageolet beans drained of liquid
4 large sprigs fresh rosemary
2 chicken stock cubes, dissolved in 900ml/
   1½ pints of water
1 tbsp tomato purée
salt and pepper

Preheat the oven to 200°C/375°F/Gas Mark 5.

1. Put the flour in a bowl, and roll each chicken thigh around in it until completely covered. Heat the oil in a shallow frying pan, and then cook each piece of chicken just until brown on each side. Put them all in a large casserole or ovenproof dish.

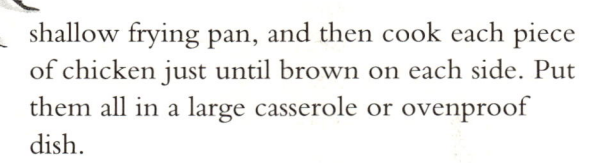

2. Chop up all the vegetables (use whatever you have at that moment, not just the ones I've mentioned) and put them in the casserole with the chicken. Add the tin of beans and stir it all together.

3. Put the fresh rosemary on top and pour over the chicken stock with the tomato purée dissolved in it. Add salt and pepper. Cover, either with a lid or with a large piece of tin foil, and bake for 2–2¼ hours.

4. Serve hot from the oven in bowls, with some boiled pasta, rice, a jacket potato, or some hot garlic bread. (Remember, garlic keeps the vampires away!)

Lemon, Banana and Poppy Seed Pound Cake

This scrumptious cake isn't full of exotic ingredients, but it can be served just as it is, and you can guarantee that everyone will like it. It's my variation on what Americans call a 'Pound Cake', meaning that it normally contains a pound in weight of every ingredient, which makes an incredibly rich and delicious cake. However, my version doesn't have a pound of everything in it, because that really does make too much, but it does have the same end result – a slightly soggy, dense cake that tastes better and better each day, and that you can still lift out of the oven! I think it works best if made either in a loaf tin or a square tin. You can serve it in big chunks, either just as it is, or if it is especially for Hallowe'en, you can make some delicious cream cheese icing, dyed red, and top each square with a disgusting jelly worm. Another alternative is to cover the whole cake in icing, and pile as many gory, revolting things on top as you like!

INGREDIENTS

3 tbsp milk
3 large eggs
1½ tsp vanilla essence
200g/7oz butter
150g/5oz caster sugar
225g/8oz plain flour
¼ tsp salt
¾ tsp baking powder
3 tbsp poppy seeds
1 tbsp grated lemon rind
2 ripe bananas, mashed

Preheat the oven to 180°C/350°F/Gas Mark 4.

1. In a small mixing bowl, combine the milk, eggs and vanilla essence.

2. In a large mixing bowl, mix the butter and sugar together with a wooden spoon. Slowly add the flour, salt and baking powder.

3. Add the egg mixture, and finally the poppy seeds, lemon rind and bananas. Beat until really well blended.

4. Grease your 22cm/9in square tin well, then spoon all the mixture in. Bake for about 1 hour depending on the shape and size of your tin, until the cake is lightly browned on top and has slightly come away from the sides of the tin.

5. Take out and leave to cool before removing the cake from the tin. Decorate as you wish, using any of the ideas I've mentioned above.

CREAM CHEESE ICING

Here's a really yummy icing recipe:

INGREDIENTS
2 × 200g/7oz packets of cream cheese
175g/6oz icing sugar
few drops of any food colouring
2 tbsp poppy seeds
1 tbsp lemon juice
½ tsp vanilla essence

Mix everything together in a bowl, until it is well blended. Spread the icing over the cake and top with any fresh fruit you like, or jelly bugs and slugs if you prefer!

My Garlic Bread

INGREDIENTS
2 cloves garlic, crushed
salt and pepper
100g/4oz butter
2 tsp any dried or fresh herbs
1 tbsp Parmesan cheese, grated (optional)
1 baguette or 4 rolls (brown or white)

Preheat the oven to 160°C/325°F/Gas Mark 3.

1. In a small bowl, mix together the garlic, salt, pepper, butter, herbs and Parmesan if you are using it. Slice the bread and spread the butter mixture in between each piece, or if you are using rolls, slice them in half and spread both halves.

2. Wrap the bread in foil, place on a baking tray and bake for 20 minutes, or until the bread looks brown and the stink of garlic is really strong!

Monster Bites

Although these biscuits are bite-size, don't be fooled into thinking that only a few will satisfy your 'monster' appetite – you will want to eat them in handfuls. They are at their best while still warm from the oven, but they will stay fresh for several days if you keep them in an airtight container. Another good idea is to make them for someone as a gift: bake them on the day, package them in a pretty box or bag, and tie with ribbon and a tag for a really thoughtful present. Believe me, giving someone something delicious to eat is the surefire way to win them over! These are chewy, gooey and great.

INGREDIENTS
(Makes about 20 biscuits)
150g/5oz demerara sugar
2 tbsp sunflower or vegetable oil
1 egg white
3 tbsp fresh orange juice
2 tsp grated orange peel
1 tbsp golden syrup
225g/8oz self-raising flour
20 hazelnuts (optional)

Preheat the oven to 180°C/350°F/Gas Mark 4.

1. Put the sugar and oil together in a bowl and beat well.

2. Add the egg white, orange juice and grated orange peel and continue to beat for a further three minutes, then add the golden syrup and beat again.

3. Stir in the flour, using a wooden spoon, until it becomes a well-blended mixture.

4. Using your hands, roll dollops of the mixture into balls and place on a greased baking sheet. Press a hazelnut in the middle of each one and bake in the oven for about 12–15 minutes, or until puffed up and golden brown.

Ghoulish Gargle
(a spooky drink)

INGREDIENTS
(Makes 4 tall glassfuls)
1 1/2 pt bottle of ginger ale
a few drops of black food dye
750ml/1/2 pt tub raspberry sorbet (or any other flavour)
225g/8oz either blueberries, raspberries or strawberries

Extras
Ice-cream scoop
Edible or plastic bugs (with plastic bugs, use only large ones that are too big to be swallowed – anything small would be very dangerous).

Put the 'bug' at the bottom of a tall glass and pour the ginger ale almost up to the top. Add a drop of food dye topped with a scoop of sorbet and a large spoonful of fruit. Then serve and watch what happens . . .

Homey Hot Chocolate

If you've just come back from a cold evening out 'trick or treating', why not simmer down with some of this really luxurious hot chocolate. It's delicious enough to warm away any shivers.

INGREDIENTS
(Makes 4 steaming mugfuls)
200g/7oz bar plain chocolate
2 tbsp honey
1/2 tsp cinnamon
1/4 tsp nutmeg
4 cupfuls of milk

1. In a double boiler or a small bowl suspended over a saucepan filled with about 5cm/2in of simmering water, melt the chocolate. Be careful not to overheat.

2. In another saucepan, heat together all the other ingredients until just about to boil. Take off the heat and stir in the chocolate using a spoon or a hand whisk. Serve immediately.

ENVIRONMENTALLY FRIENDLY PARTY

This is a very topical party, and one that I am sure everyone will be happy to participate in. We are all becoming more aware of the damage being done to the environment, so this could really be an 'environmentally aware' occasion, to remind us that we all can and should help to save our world, even if only in small ways. (Ideally, of course, *all* your parties should be environmentally friendly!)

INVITATIONS

Obviously, these have to be on recycled paper. Either cut them out in the shape of a tree, or draw the world and planets on a card with a message or quote on it from you that you think depicts the situation, such as 'Think Green!', 'Save Our Planet!' or 'Recycle It!' Or you could find an article on something to do with the environment, perhaps the rain forests or the ozone layer, and photocopy it and send it out. Alternatively, you could press some flowers or leaves, and stick them on to a piece of recycled paper like a collage.

GAMES

Have an 'environment quiz': put together a load of questions to test everyone's knowledge of how they can help the environment, to see who's clued up about what can be done to improve the situation (e.g. not using aerosols, recycling bottles and cans, etc.). You can find all the information you need in your local library.

Design a poster using things that can be recycled. Make it enormous and include messages from everyone explaining how much you care about the environment. Try to come up with a slogan for an advertising campaign – you never know, it may get put up in your school as a work of art!

Easy Tiramisu Pudding Cake

The name of this Italian dish means 'pick me up'. It is incredibly yummy and most recipes for it are very complicated, but I think I've finally managed to come up with a foolproof version. It's similar to a trifle, and you can add some fruit between the layers if you want to (raspberries work the best).

INGREDIENTS
2 packets sponge fingers
4 heaped tbsp coffee, dissolved in 2 cups hot water
6 tbsp cocoa powder
5 tbsp caster sugar
250g/9oz mascarpone cheese
50ml/2fl oz double cream
1 tsp vanilla essence

1. Take a large bowl, and line the bottom with 1 packet of the sponge fingers, which you dip in the coffee first. Save the rest for later. Sprinkle the top with some of the cocoa powder until covered.

2. In a mixing bowl, mix together the caster sugar, mascarpone, double cream and vanilla essence.

3. Spread half the cream mixture over the soaked biscuits, then make another layer – first the biscuits, then the cocoa powder, then the cream mixture. Finish off with a good sprinkling of cocoa powder and leave it covered in the fridge overnight. To decorate, you can cut out some cardboard leaves or another design out of card. Place them on the top of the tiramisu, then, using a fine sieve, sprinkle some icing sugar over the top. Carefully lift off the cards and you'll be left with the shape of the leaf.

Quick and Easy Stir Fry

If I had to recommend one item that every kitchen should have, it would be a wok. They are readily available and they really are brilliant. If you're ever stuck for an idea of what to cook, throw a few things in a wok and you'll amaze yourself with the result. You really can play around with the ingredients in this recipe. Loads of things are wonderful stir-fried; try skinned and boned duck breast, chicken breasts or prawns, and mix them with a selection of your favourite vegetables. You can add some cooked egg noodles or cooked rice at the last minute.

INGREDIENTS

3 tbsp sunflower oil (or 2 tbsp sunflower and 1 tbsp sesame oil)
2.5cm/1 in piece of root ginger, peeled and chopped
2 rump steaks, cut into strips
4 spring onions, chopped
1 red pepper, cored and seeded, thinly sliced into strips
handful of mange tout
4 sheets of egg noodles, cooked
4 tbsp of soy sauce (more or less – do it to your taste!)

1. Heat the oil in a wok or a large frying pan. Add the ginger and cook for a minute or so, then remove and throw away.

2. Add the beef strips and toss constantly around the pan until just cooked. Add the rest of the vegetables, and stir fry for 3–4 minutes until everything is just cooked but the vegetables are still crunchy.

3. Add the cooked noodles to heat through, then add soy sauce to taste and serve immediately.

Totally Green Salad

As the title suggests, you can put only green things in this salad.

INGREDIENTS

100g/4oz French beans
100g/4oz mange tout
2 large broccoli heads
1 iceberg lettuce
20 spinach leaves or roquette leaves
1 cucumber
1 green pepper
4 sticks of celery
1 green apple, chopped and cored

Simply select any or all of the above. Adjust the measurements according to what ingredients you have and how many it is for. Boil or steam French beans, mange tout and broccoli and then put them in cold water for a couple of minutes to stop them cooking any more, before adding to the chopped-up salad ingredients, so that they are cooked but still crunchy. Then drizzle over the Pesto Dressing, or any other dressing that you like on your salads.

Pesto Dressing

INGREDIENTS
2 tbsp ready-made pesto sauce
2 tbsp olive oil
juice of ½ lemon
¼ tsp black pepper
¼ tsp salt

Put all the ingredients into a clean jam jar, screw the top on tightly, and shake it all together until well blended. Store in the fridge until you need it.

Sensational Scones

INGREDIENTS
100g/4oz self-raising flour
100g/4oz wholemeal flour
50g/2oz butter or margarine
2 tsp baking powder
150ml/¼ pt milk (plus extra for glazing)

Then either of the following:
No. 1 (For savoury scones)
½ tsp mustard powder
pinch of salt
50g/2oz grated Cheddar cheese
Or:
No. 2 (For sweet scones)
50g/2oz raisins
25g/1oz caster sugar
½ tsp cinnamon

Preheat the oven to 220°C/425°F/Gas Mark 7.

1. Put all the basic scone ingredients except the milk in a large mixing bowl and mix it together using either 2 knives, your fingertips or a mixer, until it resembles fine breadcrumbs. Add the savoury or the sweet flavourings.

2. Slowly pour in the milk, little by little, mixing constantly until it all binds together.

3. Put the dough on a well-floured surface. Knead until smooth, and then pat the dough out until it is 1.25cm/½in thick.

4. Cut out the scones using a crinkly pastry cutter (or an upturned glass). Put them on to a greased baking tray, and brush with a little milk.

5. Bake them for 10–12 minutes, or until they puff up and look golden brown. Then leave to cool on a wire rack. Eat them hot or cold, split open and buttered.

N.B. The savoury ones are delicious just spread with butter, but the sweet ones are best eaten with a spoonful of jam and whipped cream for a traditional English tea.

BOXING DAY OR CHRISTMAS GET-TOGETHER

Christmas is a time when most people get together and have a party or a celebration, but just after Christmas, you may get left with that slight feeling of an anticlimax, and think that it's all gone by too quickly. You will probably feel sick to death of all that rich Christmas food – BUT, what you will also have is a fridge full of leftovers, and plenty of friends hanging around in the same position as you. What could be a better time to throw a get-together! Also, if you forgot anybody on the present list, the 'Almost Graham Crackers' would make a great present if gift-wrapped.

INVITATIONS

Buy some candy canes, tie on tags with the party details and post them, making sure they are well padded in tissues so they do not snap in the envelope. Alternatively, write down a selection of all the worst Christmas cracker jokes you've heard that year, and use them as invitations, not forgetting to write the party details on the back. If you're feeling artistic, you could draw a few bits of holly around the edge too.

GAMES

Why not have a 'Christmas Lucky Dip'? Everyone gets at least one present that perhaps they would like to swop. Get each guest to wrap theirs up in some leftover Christmas wrapping paper, bring it along to the party and put it in a large box or basket with all the others people have brought along. Add some shredded-up newspaper, and let the dip begin! Remember not to wrap up a present that someone coming to the party has given to you. Or you could host a little Christmas Quiz. Put together as many questions as you can relating to Christmas: for example – 'How many reindeer does Father Christmas have and what are their names?' or 'Name as many films and books relating to Christmas as you can'. Think of all the songs to do with Christmas, give people the opening line and let them finish it, or find out who can say 'Happy Christmas' in the largest number of different languages.

Of course, you could play more traditional Christmas games like charades or consequences – or if you're having more of a family get-together why not sing a few Christmas carols!

Turkey Burgers

A brilliant way of using up all that leftover turkey without having yet another turkey sandwich. Mix the turkey up with any leftover vegetables and you'll find yourself eating the most delicious supper.

INGREDIENTS

450g/1lb cooked turkey, finely chopped
1/2 tsp salt
1/4 tsp black pepper
1 medium finely chopped onion
900g/2lb potatoes, mashed
2 cupfuls of any leftover chopped up vegetables
2 tsp dried mixed herbs
2 eggs, beaten
4 tbsp plain flour
1 egg
4 tbsp sunflower or vegetable oil

1. Mix the turkey, salt and pepper, onion, mashed potatoes, leftover vegetables, mixed herbs and beaten eggs together in a bowl, and stir well.

2. Put the flour in one bowl, and the third egg, beaten, in another. Take handfuls of the turkey mixture and pat them into burger shapes in your hands. Dip them first into the egg, and then roll them in the flour to coat them lightly.

3. Heat the oil in a frying pan. Put the burgers in and fry for about 5 minutes on each side until golden. Serve hot with a huge salad.

N.B. You could also add some chopped ham to the recipe, or some grated courgettes, or even some chopped-up pickled onions – there's usually a jar of those in the house at Christmas.

Leftover Mashed Potato Biscuits

You might never have thought of using leftover mashed potato to make biscuits. They don't look very exciting but they have a great flavour, and are perfect as a savoury snack to eat while watching old movies over the holidays.

INGREDIENTS
(Makes about 10–12 biscuits)

175g/6oz mashed potatoes
150ml/5floz milk (plus extra for glazing)
75g/3oz wholewheat flour
100g/4oz self-raising flour
2½ tsp baking powder
1 tsp caster sugar
½ tsp salt
100g/4oz butter
100g/4oz grated Cheddar cheese
½ tsp English mustard

Preheat oven to 200°C/400°F/Gas Mark 6.

1. Grease 2 baking sheets. Put the mashed potatoes and milk into a mixing bowl and stir well.

2. In another bowl, put the two flours, baking powder, sugar and salt. Then mix in the butter with your fingertips until the mixture resembles breadcrumbs.

3. Add the potato to the flour mixture along with the cheese and mustard. Stir the whole thing really well until a very sticky dough is formed.

4. Turn the dough out on to a well-floured surface and knead for a few minutes until no longer sticky (keep adding flour as necessary). Then pat the dough out using your hands, to about 1.25cm/½in thick, and use either a pastry cutter or an up-turned glass to cut out about 10–12 biscuits.

5. Put the biscuits on the baking sheets and brush them with a little milk, using a pastry brush. Bake for about 12 minutes, or until they puff up and go golden brown (they're a little bit like scones). They taste best when served straight from the oven, but you could always re-heat them the next day if there are any left.

Almost Graham Crackers

This is my recipe for these American savoury crackers, perfect for eating with leftover cheese. I don't know why the Americans call them 'Graham Crackers' but I like the name because my husband is called Graham (although he's definitely not crackers!). They will keep for ages if you store them in an airtight container, and are great served as a savoury snack.

INGREDIENTS
(Makes about 40 crackers)
225g/8oz wholemeal flour
225g/8oz plain flour
25g/1oz caster sugar
pinch of salt
2 tbsp caraway seeds (optional)
225g/8oz butter
100ml/4fl oz double cream

Preheat the oven to 200°C/400°F/Gas Mark 6.

1. Put the flours, sugar and salt into a bowl and stir around. Add the caraway seeds here if you're using them.

2. Then add the butter, and use either your fingers or a food processor to blend it in, until the mixture resembles breadcrumbs.

3. Add the double cream, and stir until the dough binds together to form a ball.

4. Put the dough on to a really well-floured surface (it can be very sticky!) and, using plenty of flour on your hands, knead it for 2–3 minutes until smooth.

5. Roll the dough out into a rectangle about 5mm/¼in thick and, using a knife, slice into small rectangles.

6. Bake for 8–9 minutes, or until firm and golden brown, transfer to a wire rack and leave to cool completely.

Festive Fruit Salad

Make this salad to use up lots of the fresh fruits that are so good at this time of year.

INGREDIENTS
6 cupfuls of any chopped fresh fruit you like (satsumas, bananas, apples, dates, cherries, pears, plums)
6 tbsp fresh orange juice (or apple juice)
100ml/4fl oz whipping or double cream
6 tbsp demerara sugar

1. Mix together all the chopped fruit with the orange juice in a bowl. Spread the mixture out into a shallow ovenproof dish.

2. Whip the cream, spread it over the top of the fruit, sprinkle the top with the sugar, and place under a hot grill for about 5 minutes until golden. Eat immediately or refrigerate until you need it.

Italian Grilled Vegetables

Grilled vegetables have become very trendy – not only are they extremely healthy to eat, they are also easy to make and taste delicious, served either on their own, or with grilled fish or meat.

INGREDIENTS

4 tomatoes
6 mushrooms (any of the larger varieties, not button mushrooms)
3 courgettes
1 aubergine
1 red, green or yellow pepper
salt and pepper
1 tbsp dried oregano
juice of ½ lemon
4–6 tbsp olive oil

1. Put the vegetables on a good chopping surface and, using a knife, do the following:
Cut the tomatoes in half.
Slice the mushrooms into 3–4 pieces.
Chop the ends off the courgettes, and slice them lengthways into strips about 5mm/¼in thick.
Take the aubergine, cut off the ends, cut into 5mm/¼in strips, and soak in salted water for about 20 minutes before draining. Remove the seeds and cut the pepper into strips.

2. Cover a large baking tray with tin foil and place the vegetables on top. Sprinkle on the salt, pepper and oregano, squeeze on the lemon juice and finally drizzle the olive oil over the top. Place under a hot grill for about 10–12 minutes on each side.

3. These can be eaten hot or cold. If you want to eat them hot, make some bread crouton slices to put them on. Take 4 slices of brown bread, spread each side generously with butter, heat a little oil in a pan and gently fry the bread until golden brown on each side. Spread some vegetables over the top of each crouton and serve. Alternatively, make a grilled vegetable sandwich with a few of the vegetables placed between two halves of that delicious Italian ciabatta bread.

Celebration Christmas/ Boxing Day Cake

At Christmas we often eat too many sweet, sickly things such as Christmas cake and Stollen, so here's a savoury cake that's cheesy, scrummy and filled with leftover things, which makes the perfect tea-time snack. It's my version of what Italians call a *frittata*, which is a kind of omelette.

INGREDIENTS

450g/1lb long grain rice (brown or white)
100g/4oz grated hard cheese (any you like)
3 eggs
225ml/8fl oz milk
2 tbsp double cream
salt and pepper
4 slices of cooked ham, chopped
200g/7oz tin of sweetcorn or 2 cupfuls of any leftover cooked vegetables you like (broccoli, carrots, potatoes, etc.) instead of sweetcorn and courgettes
1 tsp oregano
1 tbsp vegetable oil
2 courgettes, sliced
1 medium onion, chopped

Preheat the oven to 180°C/350°F/Gas Mark 4.

1. Cook the rice first by adding it to a pan of boiling water for about 20 minutes (or 30 minutes for brown rice). Drain it and put it into a large mixing bowl with the cheese, eggs, milk, cream, salt and pepper, chopped ham, sweetcorn and oregano.

2. Heat the vegetable oil in a frying pan, and gently fry the courgettes and onion until just going brown. Drain off any excess oil and add to the rice mixture.

3. Pour the mixture into a greased 20cm/8in round cake tin and bake for 20–30 minutes until it's set (you don't want any raw egg oozing out of the middle!). Place under a hot grill for about 5 minutes until golden on top. This is best served in hot slices straight from the oven.

I don't really think this needs decorating, but if you are still in the festive mood, you could always stick some holly on the top.

OTHER INSPIRING PARTY IDEAS!

Potty Pancake Party

Welcoming Your New Baby
Brother/Sister Party

Lazy Day Party

St Patrick's Day Party

Chinese New Year Party

Pre-Lent Party – before
you give up everything!

Fourth of July
All-American Red, White and Blue Party

School Reunion Party

Favourite TV Show Party

Old Fashioned Tea Party

Totally Tacky Party!

Bon Voyage Party

Housewarming Party

Moving Away Party

Good Luck Party

Surprise Party

As you can see from the above list, you can come up with a party to suit any occasion!